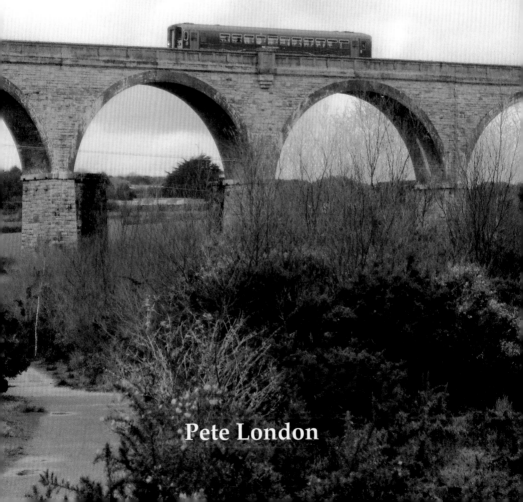

Great
Railways
of
Cornwall

Pete London

Published by Tor Mark, United Downs Ind Est, St Day, Redruth, Cornwall TR16 5HY   www.tormark.co.uk

First published 2012 © Pete London 2012: All rights reserved

ISBN 978 085025 430 3

Designed by Alix Wood www.alixwood.co.uk

Printed by R Booth Ltd, The Praze, Penryn, Cornwall TR10 8AA

Picture credits:
Cover; p5; p7; p28; p45 ©Roger Geach
p2; p27; p30; p42; p46 © ImageRail
p8 © David Letcher/Bodmin & Wenford Railway
p10; p13; p14 © Launceston Steam Railway
p15; p16; p17 © Helston Railway Preservation Society
p19; p21 © Keith Lloyd/Lappa Valley Railway
p23 © Ray Bentley/Devon & Cornwall Rail Partnership
p25 © Devon & Cornwall Rail Partnership
p29 © Lyn Winter/Devon & Cornwall Rail Partnership
p47 © Devon & Cornwall Rail Partnership - Artwork Ian Pethers

Black & white images © The Cornwall Centre, Redruth

All remaining images © author/publisher

CONTENTS

Introduction

Since 'Captain Dick' Trevithick's black *Puffing Devil* clanked up Camborne Hill on Christmas Eve 1801, Cornwall has had a close association with steam transport. During Victorian times railways flourished; a web of routes spread across the Duchy connecting towns, villages and a shoal of tiny halts. Today, though much has changed, on several lines nostalgic reminders of Cornish steam travel are still with us. The locomotives and their enthusiastic guardians keep former times alive and provide enjoyable outings for everyone.

Several scenic branch lines running regular diesel services have also survived in Cornwall, despite Dr Richard Beeching's 'axe' wielded for the Government in the 1960s, which led to cutbacks of routes throughout Britain. Rural areas were widely affected; Cornish closures included parts of the North Cornwall Railway and the West Cornwall Railway. Now though, across the Duchy five branch lines managed by operator First Great Western meander through wonderful countryside, well away from the bustle of their main-line counterparts; they offer great trips, often to places you might otherwise overlook.

All the routes allow travellers to explore the surrounding countryside and attractions. Walking trails too have been developed; station-to-station or circular, they vary from easy ambles to more challenging hikes. If you'd prefer someone else to do the driving while you discover a variety of the Duchy's most beautiful spots, make a date with Cornwall's great little railways.

Bodmin & Wenford Railway

Address:
Bodmin & Wenford Railway,
General Station, Bodmin PL31 1AQ

Location:
From Exeter take the A30 west via
Okehampton and Launceston to
Bodmin; from west Cornwall take the
A30 east; from north Cornwall take the
A39 to Wadebridge then the A389 to
Bodmin. Then follow the brown tourist
signs to Bodmin General Station, just
outside the town centre

Opening times:
Check with website

Parking:
Free parking is available on-site

Catering:
The station buffets at Bodmin General
and Bodmin Parkway serve a selection
of hot and cold snacks

Special services and events:
The Bodmin & Wenford hosts many
special events and services, virtually year-
round; for details, watch the website

Disabled facilities:
Ramps allow wheelchair access to trains,
and staff are always pleased to help out

Telephone:
Passenger enquiries 0845 125 9 678

Website:
www.bodminandwenfordrailway.co.uk

Cornwall's only full-size line still using steam locomotives is operated by the Bodmin & Wenford Railway. Run by dedicated volunteers, the track provides a round trip of thirteen miles riding in authentic wooden-panelled carriages from bygone times.

Today's route began as a Great Western Railway (GWR) link off the main Plymouth – Penzance service. A branch from the main-line's Bodmin Road (now Bodmin Parkway) was opened in 1887 to the newly-opened Bodmin station (now Bodmin General); during the following year track was laid between Bodmin and Boscarne Junction, where it joined the Bodmin & Wadebridge Railway. The service toiled through two World Wars but passenger steam trains ceased in 1963; diesels ran until 1967 and china clay freight locomotives up to 1983, when the line finally closed.

During June 1984 local enthusiasts formed the Bodmin Railway Preservation Society, their aim to re-open the line and operate steam engines; from this emerged the Bodmin and Wenford Railway group. After much fund-raising, toil on trackbed, rails and buildings, and acquisition of rolling stock helped by the Cornish Steam Locomotive Preservation Society, during June 1986 the line began short runs within the confines of Bodmin General station. Four years later timetabled passenger services commenced between General and Parkway, and in 1997 the Boscarne link was reopened.

Today, from General's single platform the line provides a choice of destination; to the west is Boscarne Junction. Passing a signal box copied from the original, the track curls round the edge of Bodmin's housing, through open fields, trackside trees and larger wooded areas, down an almost continual gradient and over the Camel River. Set in a small grove, on Boscarne's platform there's a smart stone waiting room while the single track splits into two, allowing engines to run round to the other end of the train for the return journey.

Alternatively, travelling south-east to Parkway you'll leave General for pasture and woodland, passing under the iron bridge at tiny Colesloggett Halt. Via the River Fowey crossing, the train pulls in to the main-line station's Platform 3. Both journeys last around 25 minutes; passenger trains run between February and December but take a break during November.

Most services include a buffet and bar, and the majority are steam-hauled though diesels make occasional appearances. Bodmin General has been restored to represent a station from the 1950s, with thoughtful detail: old-fashioned period signs and advertising, cast-iron lamps, wicker and leather luggage neatly stacked on hand-barrows. Sounds, smells and colours resonate; slam-doors, soot and steam, the deep greens, reds and creams of station and carriages. But centre-stage are the locomotives, from tiny Judy and Alfred late of Par Docks, low-cut to pass under the bridges there, to the Drummond T9 Greyhound built in 1899. Beattie Well tank engine No.30587, on loan from the National Railway Museum at York, served for many years on the old Bodmin and Wadebridge line.

The main station is a real Mecca for steam fans who are welcome, with permission, to visit the substantial workshop to watch restoration work on the engines. For the die-hard fanatic or those wanting to try something truly different, Bodmin & Wenford also offers spring and autumn day-long steam footplate courses. The theory of how locomotives are operated is followed

by a memorable practical experience; each student makes one journey as guard, one as fireman and one as driver.

But while steam enthusiasts are well looked after, Bodmin has also made serious efforts to broaden its appeal. Throughout the year the Railway holds themed activities: Steam and Diesel galas, Steaming Thru the '40s days, Branch Line weekends. Steam trains also host Murder Mystery evenings, Steam Beer & Jazz functions, Valentine's Night and Mothering Sunday events. For special occasions the line operates a First Class dining train and during December, Santa by Steam specials.

Aptly-named Paddington Bear, together with Fireman Sam and Postman Pat all find time in their hectic schedules to visit Bodmin, while during the summer the main station's yard hosts heritage transport festivals which include vintage cars, commercial vehicles and traction engines. Wheelchair access is widespread, on most trains there's a licensed buffet, the Railway welcomes dogs and bikes, and parking's free.

Bodmin's surroundings too provide diversions. Bodmin General is near the town's attractions: shops and cafes, a local history museum, the old gaol, the Duke of Cornwall's Light Infantry Museum. From Bodmin Parkway an old carriage-drive of around 1¾ miles, beset with rhododendrons, leads to one of the most impressive Cornish stately homes: the National Trust's Lanhydrock House.

Between General and Parkway, Colesloggett Halt makes an ideal starting-point for exploring Cardinham Woods to the north, around forty minutes' walk. At Boscarne, the recreational Camel Trail runs alongside, a favourite spot for cyclists to stop and admire the trains; the renowned Camel Valley Vineyard is close by, where guided tours are available.

For the future, the railway's custodians are hoping to extend the line from Boscarne, alongside the Camel Trail to Wadebridge. It's a substantial project, which would create a total track length for the railway's western section of just under six miles.

Launceston Steam Railway

Address:
St. Thomas Road, Launceston PL15 8DA

Location:
From the A.30 take the Launceston turning, and follow the brown tourist signs to the main railway station. From north Cornwall take the B3254, and from north Devon the A388. The railway is just outside the town centre

Opening times:
Seasonal; it's best to check with the website

Parking:
On the nearby Newport Industrial Estate, a short walk from the main Launceston station

Catering:
The main station has a buffet where a choice of hot and cold refreshments is available

Special services and events:
The line hosts visiting locomotives from other lines. Check with the website for details

Disabled facilities:
Limited, but staff are always pleased to help

Telephone:
01566 775665

Website:
www.launcestonsr.co.uk

At the Duchy's eastern end, the 2' 0" narrow-gauge Launceston Steam Railway runs on the trackbed once used by the old North Cornwall Railway, and is based at a station built from scratch over the last thirty years. Just across from the main-line original which closed in 1966, the current railway was masterminded by enthusiasts Nigel Bowman and Jim Stone, and supported by Launceston Council. Beginning at Cornwall's ancient capital, the single-track route passes though the lush green scenery of the Kensey Valley before terminating at the village of Newmills.

Launceston's beautifully restored Victorian locomotives have been brought in from the Welsh mountain railways. The first to arrive, Lilian, dates from 1883 and was rescued by Nigel Bowman during 1965. She's an 0-4-0ST Quarry Hunslet (Penrhyn Port class) built in Leeds, which during her working life toiled mostly at the Penrhyn slate quarry in Gwynedd. Lilian arrived at Launceston during 1983, today the oldest Hunslet steam locomotive still in working order; throughout her long life she's had only two owners.

In her 101st year, on Boxing Day 1983 Lilian officially opened the Launceston Steam Railway passenger service. Younger sister Covertcoat, named after the Irish horse which won the 1913 Grand National, was acquired during 1984; later she received a new tender built at the railway, to increase her coal and water capacity. Privately-owned Velinheli, 126 years old, is also a Quarry Hunslet and came to Launceston in 1986, again rescued from the Welsh slate industry, while Dorothea, essentially the same design as Covertcoat and Velinheli, features an enclosed cab.

The five-mile round trip along Launceston's scenic line operates either closed or open carriages depending on the weather, and there's a train every hour. All the carriages have been built at the railway but are based firmly on authentic designs, while wagons have arrived from a variety of sources.

The Kensey Valley's undulating meadows and woods are well worth a walk or a picnic; since the railway's tickets are flexible day-rovers you can come and go as you please, and ride as much as you like. Between Launceston and Newmills there's a request stop at the Hunt's Crossing halt, which is a good point to start discovering the surrounding countryside.

You'll also find good walking from the Newmills end of the line and leaflet guides are available, while a yomp to Tregadillet's ivy-clad Eliot Arms for a pint of real ale might take your fancy; you'll earn it, the route's a hilly one. Close to the westernmost station is New Mills Farm Park, aimed particularly at young families and including a pets' corner, ball pools, swings, slides and plenty of games.

Back at Launceston station there's a bookshop to browse, a gift area stocking souvenirs and a neatly turned-out buffet; both the buffet and the station's booking-office building started life as part of the 1919 Ideal Home Exhibition. The canopy over the platform was liberated from the old Tavistock North railway station, arriving in 1986; from times past too, the platform's ephemera includes old-fashioned lamps and signage.

Across the road from the station you'll find the Engineering Museum, where a visit really is a must. The museum houses rare machinery including vintage motorcycles, a Frazer Nash car and a Trojan van that once starred in a Disney film; also on display is an ex-Post Office underground railway train. If you're lucky or phone ahead for details, you may catch some of the exhibits being demonstrated or repaired. The museum buildings and workshop originally belonged to the local gas company.

Adding to the variety on show, engines from other lines make occasional visits. During 2009 Darjeeling Himalayan locomotive No.19 arrived at Launceston by low-loader, and a gala occasion was organised in her honour. Since then, the Andrew Barclay 0-6-0 Tank

No.1578 Gertrude has called, as well as the new-build Lyd, a replica of one of the long-lost Lynton & Barnstaple Railway Manning Wardle locomotives. The quirky Roanoke 0-4-0 vertical-boilered steam tram locomotive makes rare public appearances, though it's privately-owned and usually works on the Trevaylor Farm tramway near Truro.

Coming projects at Launceston include the construction of a diesel-electric railcar, for use during the quieter parts of the year when it's not cost-effective to run a steam train but visitors would still like to ride on the line. Built largely from scratch, the railcar will incorporate seats taken from an old Blackpool tram.

The railway is hopeful of eventually increasing the track length as far as the village of Egloskerry, around five miles north-west of the main station. In the days of the old North Cornwall Railway, Egloskerry was the next stop west from Launceston. Originally mooted as part of a multi-use recreational trail under a Cornwall Council project, funding problems have delayed the additional track. However, the Council has committed to designing the trail to allow for a future extension of the railway line when building becomes practical.

Helston Railway

Address:
Trevarno Manor and Country Estate,
Crowntown, Helston, TR13 0RU

Location:
From Helston, take the B3302 to
Penzance; at the B3303 to Camborne
turn right. Passing through Crowntown
village turn right to the Trevarno estate.
The railway is based within the estate's
grounds. From the A30 at the St Ives
(A3074) roundabout, take the B3301
to Hayle. From the centre of Hayle,
take the B3302 towards Leedstown
and Helston, then the B3303
to Crowntown

Opening times:
see the Trevarno Estate website:
www.trevarno.co.uk

Parking: Free

Catering:
Homemade refreshments are available in
Trevarno's sub-tropical Fountain Garden
Conservatory

Special services and events:
Check with the website of the Helston
Railway Preservation Society

Disabled facilities:
Disabled parking is provided; facilities
are limited on the railway, but staff are
always pleased to help

Telephone:
01326 574274 (Trevarno Estate)

Website: www.helstonrailway.co.uk

Based in the grounds of the historic Trevarno Estate at Crowntown, between Helston and Camborne, the Helston Railway Preservation Society was formed in 2002. The group's long-term plan is to restore to running order and re-open as much as possible of the old Helston Branch Line, beginning with a three-mile section between the outlying village of Nancegollan and Helston's Water-ma-Trout district just north of the town. Since 2005 when work began, volunteers have cleared and re-laid an initial half-mile section of running track.

The line at Helston dates back to 1887 when the Helston Railway Company's service opened, a stretch of nearly nine miles connecting the villages of Nancegollan and Praze with the main-line junction at Gwinear Road, between Hayle and Camborne. After many years of service though, by the 1960s as local roads improved Helston's line came under government scrutiny. Despite local opposition, in

November 1962 passenger trains ended, freight transport two years later. During 1965 the track was lifted and the track bed sold off.

Today at Trevarno though, station buildings, a platform, track, sidings and a footbridge have all been built from scratch. A shop selling souvenirs and a memorabilia exhibition are based in an adapted British Rail General Utility van; there's also an online shop. Two locomotives are currently under restoration, Ruston & Hornsby 0-4-0 diesel shunter No.327974, and an ex-British Rail Park Royal Class 103 two-car Diesel Multiple Unit, W50413 and W56169. A sister Ruston shunter, No.395305, is in working order and when not used for railway construction work offers footplate rides to the public.

The locomotives were acquired by the Helston Railway Diesel Group, founded by members of the wider Society keen to see diesels in use on the track. But for the grand opening of the Helston Railway during July 2010, the Bodmin and Wenford Railway kindly lent a steam

engine. Ex-Par Docks shunter Judy was transported to the site by low-loader where re-named Helston Phoenix for the day, she performed the first steam run down the restored line.

During 2010 too, Helston's progress was formally recognised when it received the Heritage Railway of the Year award from the Ian Allan transport publishing company. But there's still a busy time ahead and the team is always keen to recruit new helpers for clearing, track-laying, construction, and restoration of the rolling stock.

If that's not quite your thing, a visit to see what's going on is still fun and you can also take in the historic house, gardens and woodland walks. Trevarno's normal entrance fees apply, but members of the Helston Railway receive a 25% discount on production of a valid membership card. Other attractions on the estate include the National Museum of Gardening, which has one of the largest collections of garden tools and memorabilia in the country, as well as an organic herbal workshop and a playground area for young kids.

Helston's railway group is determined to acquire a steam locomotive to complement its diesels, but first a suitable shed and maintenance facilities will have to be established, together with a set of points and a dedicated siding. A second major project will see the line extended a further quarter of a mile to Truthall Halt, and the old station there rebuilt.

Lappa Valley Railway

Address:
St. Newlyn East, Newquay TR8 5LX

Location:
From the A30 take the A3075, turn-off at Coldharbour and follow the brown tourist signs. Lappa Valley is also signposted from the A30 / A3058 intersection at Summercourt, but this route is narrow

Opening times:
Check with the Lappa Valley website

Parking:
Yes, free

Catering:
The Old Forge café offers a variety of food including local produce, lunchtime meals and Cornish cream teas, to suit most tastes and ages. Three picnic areas are also provided, and picnics can be left in the site's gift shop so you don't have to lug your food around until lunchtime!

Special services and events:
Check with the website

Disabled facilities:
Allocated parking spaces. Two compartments on the steam railway have been adapted with ramps and removable seats to carry wheel-chairs. Flagstoned paths, disabled toilets

Telephone:
01872 510317

Website:
www.lappavalley.co.uk

Two of Cornwall's best-loved steam trains work on the Lappa Valley Railway, a narrow-gauge line set among woods at St Newlyn East near Newquay. Today Lappa Valley's a family activity centre with a range of attractions: wildlife, industrial heritage, nature trails. But the site's steeped in history going back to the opening of the Wheal Rose Mine in 1814.

The main mineral extracted from the killas rock at Wheal Rose was galena, sometimes called blue lead, which was smelted to produce both lead and silver. As business prospered, during 1834 its sister East Wheal Rose Mine opened. But in 1846 tragedy struck following a severe storm when the mineshafts flooded, and many miners died. Rebuilt, work continued at the site; three years later a railway line was linked to the local mineral tramway, to take the ore to Newquay harbour for shipping. The first trains were horse-drawn, but in 1874 the line was taken over by the Cornwall Minerals Railway and steam locomotives were introduced.

After mining had left Lappa Valley, during 1896 the GWR acquired the track. Tourism grew in nearby St Agnes, Newquay and Perranporth, and the route was adapted for passenger trade. Until the 1950s the branch line continued in full swing as each year thousands of holiday-makers visited, but in the face of increasing road transport its revenue fell. During February 1963, a victim of the Beeching Report, the line closed.

That might have been the end of the story, but ten years later a section of the former trackbed was bought by Eric Booth, Lappa Valley's founder and a steam enthusiast. The line was cleared, rails relaid; in 1974 the new narrow-gauge railway opened. Today a mile of steam track runs through the valley, between the car park and ticket office at Benny Halt, and the main site at East Wheal Rose.

Three locomotives trundle up and down the main 15 inch line, adored by kids of all ages; two are steam, all comparatively modern. Zebedee, an 0-6-4 pannier tank engine, was designed by David Curwen and constructed in 1974 by Severn Lamb at Stratford-upon-Avon. Stablemate Muffin is an 0-6-0 tender loco, again by David Curwen. It was built by Berwyn Engineering of Chippenham during 1967, and arrived from the Longleat Railway.

During 2011 a third loco emerged at Lappa, Lister diesel 0-4-0 Arthur dating from 1952, also acquired from Longleat and drastically rebuilt from the old Pooh engine there. Ten passenger carriages are used, manufactured locally at St Newlyn East by Jays Gates, including one First Class with wooden panels and upholstered seats – for which there's no extra charge!

Two other lines also offer rides at Lappa. Eric, named after the site's founder, runs along the 10¼ inch gauge Newlyn Halt branch line, an 0-6-0 diesel built by Alan Keef Ltd at Ross-on-Wye. The Woodland Railway is a miniature 7¼ inch track served by a model Advanced Passenger Train, powered by an 8 hp petrol engine.

Lappa's wider leisure park hosts a crazy golf course, a boating lake equipped with canoes and paddle-boats, an electric car track, a maze based on an outline of Richard Trevithick's 1804 locomotive, and play areas for small kids. There's the restored mine engine house to admire, wild flowers are prolific, while woodland walks offer chances to spot wildlife. Buzzards, ducks and woodpeckers are often around, and if you're lucky the occasional fox, stoat, or perhaps even deer.

Admission prices at Lappa include all activities except the electric cars, which are coin-operated. Special events held now and then include magic shows, competitions, and Santa Special services. If Lappa's plentiful diversions aren't enough, nearby you'll find the nine-hole St Newlyn East Golf Course. Though the trains are the stars of the show, Lappa Valley's not just a railway; for young families particularly, it's a full day out.

Tamar Valley Railway

Location:
Cornwall/Devon border, along the River Tamar

Stations:
Plymouth – Devonport – Dockyard – Keyham – St Budeaux Victoria Road – Bere Ferrers – Bere Alston – Calstock – Gunnislake

Services:
Mondays to Saturdays, reduced service on Sundays and Bank Holidays, throughout the year. For the timetable, check with the First Great Western website

Connecting services:
Plymouth main line

Parking:
Available at all stations

Refreshments:
At Plymouth

Special services and events:
Check with the website

Disabled facilities:
At the principal stations. Wheelchair access ramps are carried on the trains

Telephone:
National Rail Enquiries 08457 48 49 50

Website:
First Great Western – www.firstgreatwestern.co.uk
National Rail – www.nationalrail.co.uk

Served by the trains of First Great Western, the scenic Tamar Valley line connects Plymouth in Devon with the River Tamar's Cornish bank. The route was originally established during 1890 by the grandly-named Plymouth, Devonport and South-Western Junction Railway, and travelled as far north as Bere Alston. Cornwall's section opened in March 1908, the original terminus Callington station at Kelly Bray. Sadly, in 1966 the stretch connecting Callington was closed though the rest of the route survived the cuts; today the line ends at Gunnislake.

All told the journey takes around 45 minutes and covers a distance of some 14 miles. From the Plymouth terminus the line passes Devonport naval dockyard and Brunel's Royal Albert Bridge, before crossing the River Tavey and pressing on to the village of Bere Ferrers on the west bank. Toward the end of its journey the route bridges the Tamar into Cornwall, passing over the towering, dramatic Calstock viaduct.

▼ Calstock viaduct under **construction 23 March 1905 (Cornwall Centre)**

As the train teeters high across the viaduct's narrow trackway, on a clear day the views up and down the river are truly fabulous. Built by Lang's of Liskeard, Calstock's viaduct is 120 ft high with a length of 999 ft, arranged as 12 main arches and a thirteenth in the foundation at the Calstock side. Constructed from over 11,000 blocks of precast ferro-concrete, granite chippings were added to the mix to give an impression of stone; the project took three years to complete. Calstock village's railway station is set on a hillside curve of the track at the viaduct's northern end, and today is unmanned.

The three miles from Calstock to Gunnislake's terminus is marked by a steady upward gradient. Amid the countryside views, reminders of the Tamar Valley's industrial past can still be made out. By the time the original nineteenth-century railway arrived, the valley had long been part of the richest copper mining area in Europe, while Calstock had developed as a port shipping copper, tin and arsenic extracted from the district. Today, the route passes ruins of mine workings, chimneys, lime-kilns and a brick-works, overgrown with lush green woodland. The Tamar Valley is designated an Area of Outstanding Natural Beauty, as well as a World Heritage Site for Cornwall and West Devon Mining landscape.

Gunnislake too grew around mining but these days it's a peaceful place with cafes and restaurants offering refreshments for travellers, as well as a heritage trail around the village. On a bench in the centre sits William, a commemorative life-size sculpture of a nineteenth-century miner. There's an opportunity to explore the Old Clink, the

Pannier Market and the fifteenth-century Church of St Mary, while buses provide links to Calstock and Tavistock. A mile from the town is the Tamar Valley Donkey Park, with outdoor and indoor activities and a variety of animals to get to know.

Some of the best walks around the Tamar Valley Line are at its northern end, accessible from Gunnislake. If it's sunny, why not mix train rides with a pleasant stroll? The footpaths provide a close-up opportunity to explore the wayside and its relics of times past. As the trains are frequent you won't be stranded, and various rover-type ticket arrangements on all the scenic lines allow you to hop on and off as you wish.

Typical is the five-mile circular walk from Gunnislake station. You'll pass along the river bank and find a tiny sixteenth-century granite crossing at Newbridge, the most southerly road bridge over the Tamar until Saltash's huge suspension bridge appeared in 1961. The route then cuts inland; at Clitters Wood, eerie overgrown mining remains can be seen. A return's made via Chilsworthy Halt, part of the old railway line axed in the 1960s, and through the quiet hamlet of Delaware.

Between Calstock and Gunnislake there's a section of the Tamar Valley Discovery Trail, a network of paths linking Plymouth and Launceston and offering further exploring opportunities. But if you'd rather admire a grand estate, during the summer season the Calstock Ferry & Motor Launch Company's open wooden boat will take you the short distance down the river to Cotehele House. A Cornish Tudor residence once owned by the Edgcumbe family, the estate features beautiful formal gardens and is open all year round. After the obligatory cream tea, if conscience gets the better of you there's a walking trail back to Calstock station!

Looe Valley Line

Location:
South-East Cornwall

Stations:
Liskeard – Coombe Junction Halt – St Keyne Wishing Well Halt – Causeland – Sandplace – Looe

Services:
Mondays to Saturdays throughout the year. Reduced service on Sundays and Bank Holidays; in winter, no Sunday service. For the timetable, check with First Great Western's website

Connecting services:
Liskeard main line to Penzance and Plymouth

Parking:
Available at all stations

Disabled facilities:
At the principal stations. Wheelchair access ramps are carried on the trains

Telephone:
National Rail Enquiries 08457 48 49 50

Website:
First Great Western –
www.firstgreatwestern.co.uk
National Rail – www.nationalrail.co.uk

Situated in south-east Cornwall, the nine-mile Looe Valley branch line begins at Liskeard and for much of its journey to the coast follows the valley of the East Looe River. When passenger services first commenced during 1879 the route was named the Liskeard and Looe Railway; it began at nearby Moorswater and connected with the Liskeard and Caradon railway. In 1909 the GWR acquired the line. We're lucky it's still with us; during 1966, just two weeks before it was due to close under the Beeching cuts, its service was reprieved by then Minster of Transport Barbara Castle.

The line's single-track for its entire length. From Liskeard's terminus, because of the bearing at which the Looe line platform was built the route initially swings north, before curling round and passing under the Cornish east-west main railway line and the A.38 road. Travelling down steep gradients, the track then heads south below the Liskeard viaduct and into peaceful countryside.

Some of Looe Valley's station names bring to mind a bygone era: Coombe Junction Halt, Sandplace, St Keyne Wishing Well Halt. At Coombe Junction, which serves the nearby villages of Coombe and Lamellion, due to the old track's legacy the train negotiates a short separate stretch of line up to the tiny single platform. Here, as passengers new to the ride watch bemusedly, the guard changes the points while the driver walks to the 'rear' end of his train to make the remainder of the journey.

After a short distance following the old Liskeard and Looe Union Canal, you'll arrive at St Keyne. The station, situated among trees near a small stone road bridge, combines period-feel brown and cream livery with an old-fashioned style shelter. Causeland's station is the line's oldest, dating from when the route first opened. Serving the nearby hamlet and surrounding countryside, these days it's a request stop; if you want to join the train, put your hand out! Sandplace station too is by request.

From Sandplace the track closely follows the contours of the Looe River, passing over the northern end of the curious Terras Crossing, a causeway prone to flooding when the tide's particularly high. After a journey of around half an hour and a beautiful view across Looe's harbour you'll pull into the final station, rebuilt in recent years and five minutes' walk from the town centre. Stroll through the old-world streets, or if you have kids with you wander down to the beach by Banjo Pier and try a spot of crabbing.

All along the Looe line there's plenty to see and do. Liskeard's station is near the town centre; visit on a Thursday to take in the livestock market. There's a town museum which provides heritage trail guides, and ample cafes and restaurants for refreshments. Down the line, at St Keyne break your journey to call at the ancient holy well, with its curious legend.

St Keyne was a holy woman, beautiful and chaste, who lived in the area during the fifth century. She left her name to the local church, and to the well on which she was said to have cast a spell. During Victorian times the myth grew that if a newly-married couple drank from the well, the spouse who drank first would assume mastery in their relationship. It wasn't unusual to see young couples running up the steep hill, racing to gain dominance for their journey through life!

St Keyne's station's also said to be haunted by a ghostly bride, the spirit of a young woman who fell from the train and broke her neck. An apparition in bridal wear has been spotted on the track between St Keyne and Causeland. For a more down-to-earth experience, drop into St Keyne's Magnificent Music Machines Museum, a unique collection of phonographs and player pianos. There's even a mighty Wurlitzer organ originally from Brighton's Regent Theatre which the owner, Paul Corin, will be pleased to demonstrate for you.

At Causeland one of the old Liskeard and Looe Canal locks can still be seen, while the surrounding area is known for its birdlife. Around a mile from the station the substantial village of Duloe has a thirteenth-century church to admire, and a standing stone circle of white quartz probably dating from the Bronze Age.

Sandplace acquired its name from the old practice of spreading sea-sand across the local fields as a form of fertiliser; the sand was barged up the river from Looe, and unloaded there. Birdlife also flourishes between Sandplace and Looe, where the river begins to widen toward its mouth. Autumn, winter and the early spring are the best times to see the birds, among them curlew, dunlin and redshanks.

For walkers the Looe Valley's ideal, sheltered and largely flat, the railway providing access to various paths and trails of varying lengths. Typical is the four-miler between Causeland and Sandplace, which takes in the standing stone circle and the local church; you'll also find the point where the old canal meets the river. If you're feeling athletic the eleven-mile yomp between St Keyne and Looe takes in villages including Herodsfoot with its mining ruins, as well as riverside and woodland. But for a gentle amble try the two-mile path linking Coombe with St Keyne, mostly along tiny lanes; you'll hear just streams and birdsong.

Atlantic Coast Line

Location:
Mid-Cornwall

Stations:
Par – Luxulyan – Bugle – Roche –
St Columb Road – Quintrell Downs –
Newquay

Services:
Mondays to Saturdays throughout the
year. Reduced service on Sundays and
Bank Holidays; in winter, no Sunday
service. For the timetable, check with
the First Great Western website

Connecting services:
Truro, Plymouth

Parking:
At all stations

Refreshments:
At Newquay

Disabled facilities:
At the principal stations. Wheelchair
access ramps are carried on the trains

Telephone:
National Rail Enquiries 08457 48 49 50

Website:
First Great Western –
www.firstgreatwestern.co.uk
National Rail – www.nationalrail.co.uk

The Atlantic Coast Line links Par on the south coast with the broad sands of Newquay's holiday resort. It's a twenty-mile journey which for the most part traces an old mineral railway link. The route is marked by varied scenery across undulating moors, thick woodlands, and the alien other-world backdrop of Cornwall's china clay industry.

The line originates from the Victorian horse-drawn mineral tramway built between Par and Bugle by industrialist Joseph Treffry, who owned copper mines, granite quarries and other interests across mid-Cornwall. After Treffry's time the route was acquired by the Cornwall Minerals Tramway, established in 1873 at St Blazey; new tracks were added for its eighteen tank locomotives, and various connecting lines appeared. Later that year the route reached Newquay and during July 1876 passenger services began. In the following year operations came under the GWR, and during 1892 the track was converted from broad to standard gauge; much of the route remains as the basis of the Atlantic Coast service.

Today from Par's Platform 3 terminus, passing Cornwall's oldest signal box the line heads sharp clockwise and then, initially, through scruffy territory. Passing St Blazey's old freight yard and its abandoned station, on the left a listed Victorian engine roundhouse survives, now industrial units. But the countryside's soon reached; curving north-west of St Blazey the line winds through woodland, at times near the Par River, up the Pont's Mill gradient, via a short tunnel to the village of Luxulyan and its spruce station.

Continuing west across moorland you'll head into the heart of the Duchy's china clay country. The clay deposits found in mid-Cornwall have been worked since the eighteenth century, their impact profound on the region's economy and physical appearance. To the left, dominating the skyline you'll see huge spoil tips tiered and pointed, mountains softened with thin grass or rudely kaolin-white. Sometimes they're called the Cornish Alps, the landscape surreal and luminescent.

Bugle and Roche sit close by Cornwall's peaks, both villages former stopping points on the old mineral line and today served by railway request stops. In fact Roche's tiny station is north of the village, closer to nearby Victoria. Heading west from Roche over the moorland of Tregoss, shortly Iron Age hill-fort Castle-an-Dinas appears, three huge concentric stone-and-earth ramparts and ditches built seven hundred feet above sea level. The flat scrub of Goss Moor nature reserve follows before the line passes under the A.30 and heads for St Columb Road station, some three miles from the village of St Columb Major itself. It's a bleak windswept place, one platform maintained but a second long derelict.

Via a short tunnel and a cutting, the line undergoes a mood-swing as Quintrell Downs' tiny station appears, the miniature section merrily reminiscent of Chigley. The fifty-minute ride ends as you cross the Trenance viaduct and enter Newquay's busy terminus. During the holiday season, as well as the local service Newquay handles various intercity trains. On summer Saturdays local trains are replaced by First Great Western services from London Paddington, as well as CrossCountry trains from the Midlands and north of England, which don't stop at stations between Newquay and Par.

Each year tens of thousands of holidaymakers visit Newquay for its huge beaches, wild Atlantic breakers and equally pounding nightlife. Activities are numerous: boating, fishing, a zoo, various adrenalin sports. But if peace and quiet is more your thing, a short walk from the station takes you to the serenity and colour of Trenance Gardens.

Chief among the Atlantic Line's areas to explore is the Luxulyan Valley, just south of the village. Today its steep green slopes are thickly wooded but during the nineteenth century Joseph Treffry's mines and quarries were in full swing, the area industrialised on a vast scale. To carry his horse-drawn tramway over the valley Treffry built a great granite viaduct 650 feet long, 100 feet high, with ten arches each spanning 40 feet, at the time the largest in the south-west

▼ Having dropped its passengers the Par train reverses out of Newquay station sometime in the mid 1950s. Newquay retains its very long platforms to accommodate intercity trains on summer Saturdays (ARTHUR TREVENNA COLLECTION — CORNWALL CENTRE)

of Britain. Opened in 1842 it's still there, today a monument to Cornish engineering skills, and the railway passes underneath.

In fact industrial archaeology is scattered throughout the valley; as well as the viaduct a canal, a waterwheel pit, leats and tracks can be found, ruins gently reclaimed by nature and accessible to walkers. The surroundings are tranquil, lush from the waterways' moisture, visitors surprisingly few. Treffry's viaduct comes under the protection of the Cornwall Heritage Trust and is a Scheduled Ancient Monument. A group of volunteers, The Friends of Luxulyan Valley, work to preserve the surroundings; their guide book's available in the village and is invaluable for visitors wishing to understand the area's history. Another good reason to call in at Luxulyan is the pub, which serves excellent beer and food – the writer has diligently checked out both.

At Roche too there's history but in a quite different form. Atop a vertigo-inducing granite outcrop east of the village sits a ruined fifteenth-century chapel, surrounded by myth and fable. Did star-crossed Arthurian lovers Tristan and Iseult take shelter at the site? Some say a hermit lived in the chapel, others that Cornwall's most evil man, attorney Jan Tregeagle, hid there from the hounds of hell sent to drag him to the depths. One thing's for sure; if you can brave the height, the view's magnificent across mid Cornwall.

Maritime Line

Location:
Central south Cornwall

Stations:
Truro - Perranwell - Penryn - Penmere - Falmouth Town - Falmouth Docks

Services:
Mondays to Saturdays throughout the year. Reduced service on Sundays and Bank Holidays; in winter, no Sunday service. For the timetable, check with the First Great Western website

Connecting services:
Penzance, Plymouth

Parking:
At all stations

Refreshments:
At Truro

Disabled facilities:
At the principal stations. Wheelchair access ramps are carried on the trains

Telephone:
National Rail Enquiries 08457 48 49 50

Website:
First Great Western –
www.firstgreatwestern.co.uk
National Rail – www.nationalrail.co.uk

Connecting Cornwall's elegant capital Truro with the huge natural port of Falmouth is the Maritime Line, a ride of around twelve miles. Originally built by the Cornwall Railway, the route opened in 1863 after Falmouth people had lobbied for a link to the Truro main-line, and thence to Plymouth. During 1889 the GWR took over the service and soon converted it from broad to standard gauge.

Today, leaving Truro's bay platform the journey to Falmouth takes around twenty-five minutes. For the first half-mile the train uses the Penzance main line, but after Penwithers junction the route is single-track all the way to Falmouth's terminus, except for a passing point at Penryn. Tunnels feature twice; the first and smaller, Highertown, is just outside Truro. Beyond a small nature reserve Sparnick Tunnel is entered, over a quarter of a mile in length. As the line turns south high above silted-up Restronguet Creek it crosses Carnon Viaduct, which allows a fine view of the surrounding countryside. Below the viaduct, perpendicular to the line runs the Mineral Tramway heritage trail connecting Devoran in the south with the north coast's Portreath, enjoyed by walkers and cyclists.

Perranwell's station buildings and restored artefacts evoke earlier times, though the platform's tiny shelter is a modern reproduction of an older style. Passing over further viaducts at Perranwell, Ponsanooth – the journey's tallest – and Penryn, as you approach Falmouth the Maritime Line provides striking outlooks across the Fal estuary. Penryn's original Collegewood Viaduct was the last timber-spanned railway viaduct built in Cornwall and was designed by Isambard Kingdom Brunel; its stone and masonry replacement was constructed during 1934, though the original piers still stand. Penryn's Jacobean and Georgian buildings are worth a quick look, particularly the unusual Town Hall.

Falmouth hosts three stations in quick succession; Penmere serves the western residential area. The station's notable for the work of the Friends of Penmere Station, a group of railway and gardening

▲ Perranwell station in the 1890s: note the raised signal box. Due to lack of space a siding ran underneath. This was thought to be one of only a handful of raised signal boxes in the country – alas destroyed long ago (CORNWALL CENTRE)

enthusiasts formed in 1993. They've transformed the station with colourful flowers and shrubs, restored GWR platform furniture, and at the entrance a jolly model locomotive overflowing with vivid blooms. Their work has been recognised by National Rail and Britain in Bloom awards.

Toward the journey's end, Falmouth Town station sits at the southern part of the commercial area; the terminus at Falmouth Docks is handy for the seaside as well as outlooks across the harbour. Falmouth teems with things to do. Along the front are several family beaches and public gardens; overlooking the coastline is Pendennis Castle, one of Britain's finest surviving Tudor fortifications and beautifully preserved. From Pendennis you can see across the wide Carrick Roads to its cousin, St Mawes Castle.

By the water too you'll find the award-winning National Maritime Museum, which brings to life the story of Britain's nautical tradition using an astonishing collection of historic and contemporary craft. The museum is fun for all ages, with children being particularly well catered for. Other local water-based activities include sailing regattas and boat hire, as well as a wide choice of scenic trips on the first-class river transport system.

The town also has a rich artistic heritage; many prominent painters past and present have been attracted to Falmouth, which today hosts several contrasting art galleries. A shoal of cafes and restaurants provide cuisine to suite all tastes and pockets, while the small independent shops, narrow alleys and old buildings make enjoyable exploring.

Truro too has plenty to see. The three-spired cathedral's a magnificent building, its stained glass and Father Willis organ truly world-class; guided tours are available and a warm welcome is extended to all. A leading custodian of Cornish heritage is the Royal Cornwall Museum, which holds outstanding art and archaeological

▲ Penryn viaduct in the early 1900s; note the wooden structure which amazingly lasted until 1923 when replaced by an embankment. Nearly all the viaducts in Cornwall were originally wooden to cut costs (ARTHUR TREVENNA COLLECTION-CORNWALL CENTRE)

collections; throughout the year too, special events are held. The Hall for Cornwall is the Duchy's principal theatre and concert venue while Lemon Quay's square hosts various themed markets, often offering local produce. After you've sauntered round the shops there are several parks and gardens to visit, and a wide choice of eateries.

As well as the two main centres, from the Maritime Line's other stations there are opportunities to explore on foot. Perranwell village provides an accessible stroll: peaceful lanes, bridleways and farms. Alternatively, from the village a longer walk down the hill leads to a stretch of the old mineral tramway's heritage trail. You'll encounter views across the woodland, ponds and heathland of the Bissoe Valley; further on, pass under the Carnon Viaduct and admire its nine great arches towering into the air.

From Falmouth Town station there's a circular walk which links Pendennis Castle and the Maritime Museum. If you want to look round both, it's best to set aside all day. Alternatively, waterfront fish-and-chips sat in the sun makes for a lazy, peaceful time – but mind the greedy Falmouth gulls!

St Ives Bay Line

Location:
Penwith

Stations:
St Erth - Lelant Saltings - Lelant - Carbis Bay - St Ives

Services:
Mondays to Saturdays, reduced service on Sundays and Bank Holidays, throughout the year. For the timetable, check with the First Great Western website

Connecting services:
from St Erth, to Penzance and Truro

Parking:
Available at all stations. Park-and-ride at Lelant Saltings for St Ives. Limited parking spaces at Lelant

Refreshments:
At St Erth

Disabled facilities:
At the principal stations. Wheelchair access ramps are carried on the trains

Telephone:
National Rail Enquiries 08457 48 49 50

Website:
First Great Western – www.firstgreatwestern.co.uk
National Rail – www.nationalrail.co.uk

Westernmost of Cornwall's scenic railways, the First Great Western's St Ives Bay Line links the village of Rose-an-Grouse, just off the A30 near St Erth, with the glorious beaches of Carbis Bay and St Ives. The line dates from 1874 when the GWR began construction; three years later the track was complete, running along a newly-built embankment at the mouth of the Hayle River, and over the handsome granite Carbis Bay viaduct. The route was the final broad-gauge passenger railway built in Britain, and like many others was converted to standard gauge in 1892. At first the railway transported fish, mostly pilchards caught by local boats, but as St Ives' fishing industry declined tourists started to use the line. Artists too began to arrive, seeking serenity as well as the brilliance and clarity of the light in West Penwith.

During the 1960s the railway came under Government scrutiny and was considered for closure, but though St Ives station lost its goods sidings the passenger line was reprieved; by then it had appeared in the song *Slow Train*, by Flanders and Swann. End to end the journey's only around four miles long and takes just twelve minutes, but the views really are delightful. The line's single-track along its entire length with no passing points. At the height of the holiday season a four-carriage train trundles back and forth, but through the winter months two cars are sufficient.

Built in 1852 by the West Cornwall Railway and originally known as St Ives Road, St Erth station is still old-fashioned, its Grade II listed buildings a comfortable reminder of times past. Today the station boasts a buffet chosen as a favourite track-side tearoom in a top-ten list published by the *Guardian*. Leaving St Erth and heading north, initially the line passes under the main A.30 road before escaping to the enchanting estuary of the River Hayle, following close by its western bank.

Lelant Saltings is the first stop, a tiny single-platform station opened during 1978, with a huge car park providing a park-and-ride facility for visitors to St Ives. A quarter of a mile along the embankment at the village of Lelant is a second unmanned station; like the Saltings it overlooks the estuary and in the background, the town of Hayle. Car parking is lacking at Lelant and the station is a request stop. Despite its sparse services though the smaller station's well worth visiting especially at low tide, since it's possible to safely cross the line there; the river bank's accessible and makes a pleasant walk.

The Hayle estuary is an RSPB nature reserve, which offers a great pause in your journey. Birdlife's present throughout the year, mostly waders and seabirds though occasionally peregrine falcons and ospreys appear. Oystercatchers, curlews and little egrets thrive, while during the spring and autumn migrating birds gather; dunlins, ringed plovers and bartailed godwits. Later in the year wigeons and

▼ Over a hundred years separate these two images, taken from almost the same place; the steam train was photographed in May 1905 (CORNWALL CENTRE)

teals collect in their hundreds. The Hayle's also home to the stately grey heron and the big cheerful-looking shelduck; more than 270 bird species have been recorded there.

As the line turns west toward St Ives, into view comes the glorious beach at Porth Kidney. Above the dunes, perched on the cliff top is the church of St Uny with its gothic graveyard of moss-covered crosses; the railway traces the cliff edge, close by Cornwall's Coastal Path with beautiful sea views. At Carbis Bay again the station's resources are modest, the small car park at the top of a slope, a single platform below. On the other hand, just across the way the beach is one of Cornwall's finest, wide and sheltered with food outlets and summer lifeguards.

Toward St Ives you'll cross over the three high piers of Carbis Viaduct before approaching the end of the line. St Ives' station is situated by Porthminster beach; its car park was built on the site of the original station and the town's a short walk away. Arriving by rail certainly provides a more restful experience than driving, especially during the summer, while the views east to Godrevy lighthouse and west as you approach St Ives simply aren't to be had from the road.

Around the stations there's much to enjoy on foot; their proximity to one another allows comfortable walking between them and the going's generally flat. The footpath from Lelant to Carbis Bay passes the RSPB reserve and the high grassy dunes of Carrack Gladden headland at the mouth of the Hayle, then along the western path low cliffs to the beach. From Carbis Bay's broad sands it's just over a mile to Porthminster beach.

Rain or shine, at St Ives there's plenty to see and do. Absorb the cobbled streets and tiny cottages, the waterfront, eateries and stone harbour piers where small boats shelter. Numerous sub-tropical gardens flourish in the mild climate and St Ives has several beaches, but if the weather changes you can experience the town's long-established reputation as a centre for the arts. There are shops, galleries and studios to enjoy, as well as the Tate Gallery which incorporates the Barbara Hepworth Museum. St Ives is also home to the re-opened Leach Pottery, perhaps the most famous and influential studio pottery in the world.

All five of Cornwall's First Great Western branch lines have nearby Rail Ale Trails, so you can combine your journey with breaks to sample the local brews. You'll find traditional, out-of-the-way pubs you wouldn't otherwise have discovered, and for souvenir hunters there are various collectibles on offer as you build up your visits. Most of the pubs serve food, and as well as their usual beers many feature guest ales; the Rail Ale Trail's website has full details of what's on offer.

More Information

For more information on opportunities to enjoy Cornwall's steam and scenic branch lines, check out these websites:

Bodmin & Wenford Railway:
www.bodminandwenfordrailway.co.uk
Fal River Links:
www.kingharryscornwall.co.uk
First Great Western train timetables:
www.firstgreatwestern.co.uk
Great Scenic Railways of Devon and Cornwall, and the Devon and Cornwall Rail Partnership **www.greatscenicrailways.com**
The Devon & Cornwall Rail Partnership was formed in 1991 to improve local railway services and promote travel on rural branch lines
Helston Railway: **www.helstonrailway.co.uk**
Lappa Valley Railway: **www.lappavalley.co.uk**
Launceston Steam Railway: **www.launcestonsr.co.uk**
Rail Ale Trail: **www.railaletrail.com**
Walking trails and guides: **www.trailsfromthetrack.com**

Acknowledgements

The writer would like to thank the following people and organisations for their generous help in connection with this book: Rebecca Catterall (Development Officer, Devon & Cornwall Rail Partnership), Roger Geach, Rachel Griffiths (ImageRail), Richard Jones (Bodmin and Wenford Railway), Keith Lloyd (Lappa Valley Railway), Charlie O'Mahoney (Launceston Steam Railway), and Stuart Walker (Helston Railway Preservation Company Limited)